To the reader:

Welcome to the DK ELT Graded Reac
different. They explore aspects of the v   ...
history, geography, science ... and a lot ... ᴜᴛʜer things. And
they show the different ways in which people live now, and
lived in the past.

These DK ELT Graded Readers give you material for
reading for information, and reading for pleasure. You are
using your English to do something real. The illustrations
will help you understand the text, and also help bring the
Reader to life. There is a glossary to help you understand the
special words for this topic. Listen to the cassette or CD as
well, and you can really enter the world of the Olympic
Games, the *Titanic*, or the Trojan War ... and a lot more.
Choose the topics that interest you, improve your English,
and learn something ... all at the same time.
Enjoy the series!

To the teacher:

This series provides varied reading practice at five levels of
language difficulty, from elementary to FCE level:
BEGINNER
ELEMENTARY A
ELEMENTARY B
INTERMEDIATE
UPPER INTERMEDIATE
The language syllabus has been designed
to suit the factual nature of the series, and
includes a wider vocabulary range than is
usual with ELT readers: language linked
with the specific theme of each book is
included and glossed. The language
scheme, and ideas for exploiting
the material (including the recorded
material) both in and out of class are
contained in the Teacher's Resource Book.
We hope you and your students enjoy using
this series.

LONDON, NEW YORK, MUNICH, PARIS,
MELBOURNE, DELHI

Originally published as Dorling Kindersley
Reader *Born to Be a Butterfly* in 2000,
text © Karen Wallace, and
adapted as an ELT Graded Reader
for Dorling Kindersley by

studio cactus C

SOUTHGATE STREET WINCHESTER HAMPSHIRE SO23 9DZ

Published in Great Britain by
Dorling Kindersley Limited
80 Strand, London WC2 0RL
A Penguin Company

2 4 6 8 10 9 7 5 3

Copyright © 2000
Dorling Kindersley Limited, London

All rights reserved. No part of this publication
may be reproduced, stored in a retrieval system,
or transmitted in any form or by any means,
electronic, mechanical, photocopying, recording,
or otherwise, without the prior written permission
of the copyright owner.

A CIP catalogue record for this book is
available from the British Library.

ISBN 0-7513-2935-5

Colour reproduction by Colourscan, Singapore
Printed and bound in China by
L. Rex Printing Co., Ltd
Text film output by Chimera.trt, UK

The publisher would like to thank the following
for their kind permission to reproduce their photographs:
c=centre; t=top; b=below; l=left; r=right

Aquila: Michael Edwards 4 inset, Anthony Cooper 29t; **Bruce
Coleman Collection:** 4–5, 7b, 8, 9, 10t, 12–13, 16–17, 18–19,
Andrew Purcell 14–15, Jane Burton 20, Kim Taylor 22–23; **Dorling
Kindersley:** Colin Keates 5 inset; **Natural History Photographic
Agency:** E.A. Janes 11, Stephen Dalton 21r; **Oxford Scientific
Films:** J.S. & E.J. Woolmer 10b; **Premaphotos Wildlife:** 25, Ken
Preston-Mafham 29c; **Richard Revels:** 7t, 28–29; **RSPCA
Photolibrary:** Jonathan Plant 6, E.A. Janes 30–31; **Windrush
Photos:** Dennis Green 24, Frank Blackburn 26–27
Jacket: **Aquila:** l; **Anthony Cooper; Telegraph Colour Library:** r
All other images © Dorling Kindersley.
For further information see: www.dkimages.com

see our complete catalogue at
www.dk.com

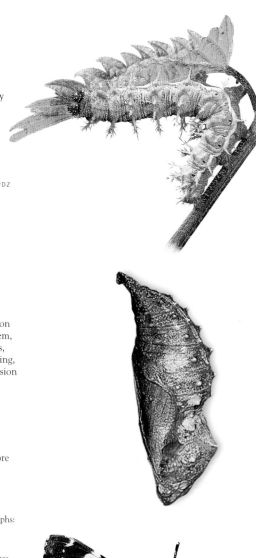

ELT Graded Readers

ELEMENTARY A

BUTTERFLIES

Written by Sarah Woolard

Series Editor Susan Holden

A Dorling Kindersley Book

A butterfly is moving from flower to flower, and its red-striped wings are shining in the sun. It looks beautiful. Maybe it is the most beautiful insect in the world. It is touching the flowers with its feet and its feelers (*long, thin hairs on its head*). What is it doing? It is looking for leaves where it can lay its eggs.

wings

Butterflies live almost everywhere in the world, and there are about 20,000 different kinds. The biggest butterfly is about 28 centimetres across, and the smallest one is only one centimetre. They have thin, smooth bodies.

feelers

Most butterflies fly during the day. They stop on flowers and leaves. When they land on a leaf, they usually point their wings up.

The butterfly is flying from leaf to leaf. It is testing them. It stops for a short time on different leaves, and then tastes them.

The butterfly lays one or two eggs on each good leaf. The outside of the egg is quite hard – it has a thin shell. The butterfly pushes a special liquid out of its body onto the eggs at the same time. This holds the eggs onto the leaf. Then it flies onto the next flower or leaf.

shell

The inside of the egg is very soft.
A caterpillar is growing inside
this egg. It is soon ready to
hatch. The eggs of some
butterflies hatch in two or three
days, but others are much slower
and hatch after six months.

caterpillar

When the caterpillar is ready to hatch, it bites through the shell with its strong, sharp teeth and moves out onto the leaf. The caterpillar is always hungry. Its first meal is usually the shell from the egg. Then it starts eating all the leaves around it. And it can eat a lot! In one day, a caterpillar can eat many times its own weight in food.

The caterpillar is growing bigger and fatter.
This is a dangerous time, because
a caterpillar is good to eat.
Sometimes it hides under
a big leaf and pulls
the leaf
around it.

Inside this leaf, the caterpillar is safe. The hungry
birds can't see it, and they can't eat it.

This caterpillar is not alone. The mother butterfly laid hundreds of eggs on the leaves all around it, and now hundreds of caterpillars are hatching out.

Some of them are lucky – they will sit in the leaves and grow big. But others will be unlucky – they make a tasty dinner for other insects and birds. Hungry birds and spiders eat them during the day, and bats eat them at night.

The hungry caterpillar can't stay inside the leaf for a long time because it soon feels hungry again. So it moves away from the leaf and starts to climb along the plant. It climbs up the strong stems and onto the young leaves. Young leaves taste very nice, and the caterpillar eats all the leaves it can find – and all the time it eats, it gets bigger and bigger. A caterpillar is a kind of moving, eating machine – it is like a huge stomach on legs! Its body is perfect for this.

A caterpillar's body has 14 sections. The first part is the head, with a mouth and six small eyes on each side. These help the caterpillar to see the difference between dark and light. The caterpillar's stomach is in ten of the sections, and it has legs on every part of its body.

Munch!
Crunch!

The caterpillar eats more and more, and gets bigger and bigger. But its skin doesn't grow bigger – this stays the same size. This soon becomes a problem. The caterpillar's black and yellow skin gets tighter and tighter. It is difficult for the caterpillar to eat. Suddenly, the skin starts to break open along its back. It looks as if the caterpillar is breaking into two pieces!

skin

Before the skin breaks open, the caterpillar grows a new skin under the old one. Then it moves out of the old skin. But the new skin is still very soft, and at first it is difficult for the caterpillar to move. It must wait. For a few hours, the caterpillar sits quietly on the leaf and its new skin gets hard. Then it is ready to start eating again.

The caterpillar grows bigger and bigger and, as it grows, it changes its skin four or five times. Then it is ready for the next stage of its life. There is just one more stage before it becomes a butterfly. Usually, it finds a safe place high up on a leaf. Then it puts a special, sticky liquid on the leaf. This helps the caterpillar to hold on (or it could easily fall to the ground). The caterpillar in this picture is getting ready for this change.

The caterpillar moves out
of its old skin for the last
time and looks for a
strong leaf, high on
the plant. Then it
uses its special,
sticky liquid. It
holds onto the leaf
and hangs upside-
down on it, with its
head at the bottom.

The next stage in the caterpillar's life is beginning: it is changing into a chrysalis. At first, the chrysalis is soft, but soon its skin becomes hard, like a shell. This keeps it safe from other insects and birds.

chrysalis

Inside this hard "shell", something amazing is happening. The chrysalis is changing into something completely different.

With some types of butterflies, the chrysalis stays inside its shell for only a few days. With other types it stays there all winter, and waits for the warm weather in the spring.

Then, one day, the chrysalis breaks open, and something comes out into the sunshine. First you can see the head, then the legs, then the whole body. It isn't a caterpillar now – it looks very different.

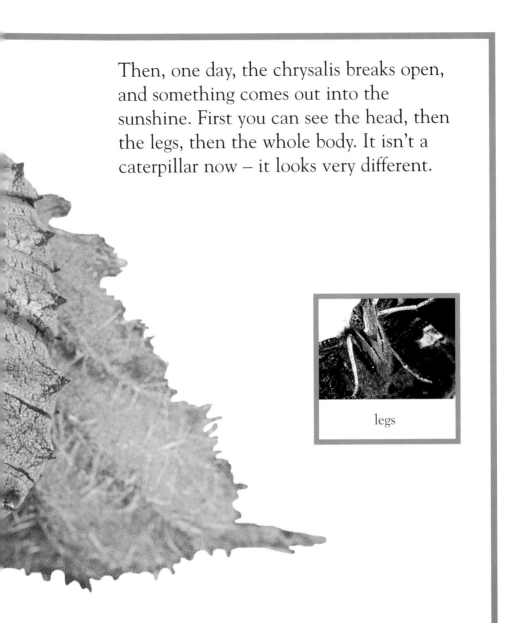

legs

It has a head and six legs. It has wings and a body. The caterpillar is now an adult. It's a butterfly.

The new butterfly rests and waits in the sunshine. At first, its body is soft and its wings are wet. It can't fly. Soon, however, its skin gets hard and the butterfly can push air and blood through its body and wings.

When it grows a little stronger, the butterfly starts to move. First, it opens its wings a little to help them to dry faster. Then, after about one hour, the butterfly is ready to fly.

When its wings are dry, the new butterfly moves from flower to flower. It drinks the nectar from the flowers with its long tongue. The butterfly pushes this long tongue into the flowers and sucks up nectar. When the butterfly is not eating, it curls its tongue up inside its mouth.

tongue

Sometimes the butterfly rests on a tree with its wings together. These are brown, the same colour as the tree. It is difficult for hungry birds to see it and eat it.

Butterflies are beautiful, but they have many enemies, and many other insects and birds like to eat them.

This butterfly is female, and now it is time for her to look for a mate. Butterflies send out signals when they are ready to mate. They use the colours in their wings and a special smell.

The male and female butterflies dance in the sunshine and fly away together. Usually, the male butterfly dies soon after mating. The female butterfly will start to lay her eggs.

Now the story begins again. The female butterfly moves from flower to flower, and its red-striped wings shine in the sun. It looks beautiful – maybe the most beautiful insect in the world.

It is looking for good leaves where it can lay its eggs, and it stops for a short time on many different leaves. It tastes them, and stops on the best ones.

Soon, there will be caterpillars on the leaves, and then there will be hundreds more butterflies, flying in the sun.

Glossary

amazing
Something that is very surprising.

bat
An animal like a mouse with wings. It flies at night.

to break
To come open suddenly, into several parts.

caterpillar
The young butterfly – like a small worm with legs.

to climb
To go up something.

to curl (up)
To make a tight, circular shape.

to dance
To move around – usually to music.

during
In this time.

enemy
The opposite of friend; something that is a danger.

to hang
To hold on at the top, so the bottom part is free.

to hatch
When a young bird or insect comes out of its egg.

to hide
To go somewhere where no one can see you.

insect
A small living creature with six legs and a three-part body.

to land (on)
To stop flying through the air, and to stand on something.

to lay eggs
To make eggs, or push the eggs out of the body.

leaf (plural – leaves)
Leaves are the flat, green parts of a tree or plant.

liquid
Water, milk, petrol are all liquids.

mate (n)
Someone or something of the opposite sex to have babies with.

to mate
To come together as male and female to make babies.

nectar
The sweet, sticky liquid in flowers.

to rest
To relax, stop working or moving.